AF333663

MIAMI DOLPHINS

THE MIAMI DOLPHINS
SUPER BOWL CHAMPIONS

JULIAN MAY

CREATIVE EDUCATION, INC.
MANKATO, MINNESOTA 56001

PHOTOGRAPHIC CREDITS

John E. Biever: 19, 23; Vernon J. Biever: 18 (top, bottom), 25, 34, 37, 40, 46; Miami Herald: 14; National Football League: 18 (center); United Press International: 2-3, 9, 10, 12, 16, 17, 20, 22, 24, 26-27, 28, 30-31, 32, 36, 39, 41, 43, 44-45, 47; Wide World: 6, 8, 13, 42.
Cover: United Press International.

Library of Congress Number: 74-4139   ISBN: 0-87191-328-3

Published by Creative Education, Mankato, Minnesota 56001
Distributed by Childrens Press, 1224 West Van Buren Street, Chicago, Illinois 60607

LIBRARY OF CONGRESS CATALOGING IN PUBLICATION DATA

May, Julian.
  The Miami Dolphins.

  (Superbowl champions)
  SUMMARY: Describes the Dolphins' push for and eventual success in winning the Superbowl two years in a row.
  1. Miami Dolphins (Football club)—Juvenile literature. [1. Miami Dolphins (Football club) 2. Football] I. Title.
GV956.M47M49   796.33'264'09759381   74-4139
ISBN 0-87191-328-3

MIAMI DOLPHINS

TWO-TIME SUPER LOSER

Coach Don Shula stood on the cold, windy sidelines and watched the opening kickoff of Super Bowl VI.

It was the first world championship game played by his young team, the Miami Dolphins. But unlike the team, the coach had been in the Super Bowl before.

Three years ago, Don Shula had coached the Baltimore Colts in Super Bowl III—and lost. Now he was back with a new team and new hope.

Miami Dolphins' coach Don Shula (right) and his quarterback, Bob Griese, before Super Bowl VI.

It was the Miami Dolphins versus the Dallas Cowboys. Dallas had lost Super Bowl V the previous year by only 3 points. This year they were strong and eager.

Don Shula smiled as Miami's fleet Mercury Morris caught the kickoff on the 6 and returned it all the way to the Dallas 26. Miami fans cheered.

Shula sent in the Dolphin offense. Quarterback Bob Griese was the best passer in the AFC. On the first play, he sent a pass to wide receiver Howard Twilley, running a down-and-in pattern.

Griese missed.

On the next Miami series, star running back Larry Csonka fumbled a simple hand-off. It was his first fumble of the season—and it led to a Dallas drive that resulted in a field goal.

Running back Larry Csonka (39) drops the handoff from Bob Griese (12) in Super Bowl VI.

Dallas Cowboy Bob Lilly (74) throws Griese for a huge loss as the first period of Super Bowl VI ends. At left is Cowboy Larry Cole (63).

As the first quarter ended, Griese dropped back to pass on third and nine. Cowboy defensive tackle Bob Lilly clobbered him for a 29-yard loss.

It was plain to Coach Shula that his young team was suffering a bad case of Super Bowl nerves!

They tried to pull themselves together in the second period. Dolphin kicker Garo Yepremian tried to tie the score with a long boot. He had led the NFL in kicking and scoring that season.

But this time he missed.

Dallas went on a 76-yard drive. They seemed cool and in control. With less than 2 minutes left in the half, the Cowboys scored a touchdown. The kick was good and the score was Dallas 10, Miami 0.

Dolphin pride demanded that they not be scoreless at the half. They had no choice but to pass.

Griese connected with Paul Warfield, Jim Kiick and Jim Mandich. The Dolphins made it to the Dallas 47 with only 22 seconds left in the half.

Then Griese threw 23 yards to Warfield. His next pass was incomplete, so Garo Yepremian came in again. In the last 8 seconds, he kicked a field goal. At the half, the score was 10-3.

Garo Yepremian (1) scores Miami's only Super Bowl VI points with a 31-yard field goal in the second quarter. Cliff Harris of the Cowboys tries to block it. Larry Csonka is at right.

Dallas runner Duane Thomas (33) leaves a host of Dolphins in his wake as he scores a second touchdown for the Cowboys. Falling by the wayside are Nick Buoniconti (85), Doug Swift (59) and Jake Scott (13). Looking on are Jim Riley (70) and Mike Kolen (57).

"It isn't hopeless!" Don Shula told his men. "We have to hold them and stop those runs up the middle. Then we can get our offense going."

It seemed like good strategy. But Dallas coach Tom Landry guessed that Shula would strengthen the middle. He sent his runners outside. The Cowboys rolled downfield for six minutes and scored another touchdown. With the point-after, it was 17-3.

The Dolphins got the ball only three times in the third quarter. They failed to score a single first down.

In the fourth quarter, a Griese-to-Kiick pass was intercepted by Cowboy linebacker Chuck Howley—the same man who had grabbed Csonka's fumble.

Howley's play ruined Miami's drive and set up another Dallas touchdown three plays later. Miami was crushed. The final score in Super Bowl VI was Cowboys 24, Dolphins 3.

And Coach Don Shula found that he was football's first two-time Super Loser. He had never felt lower.

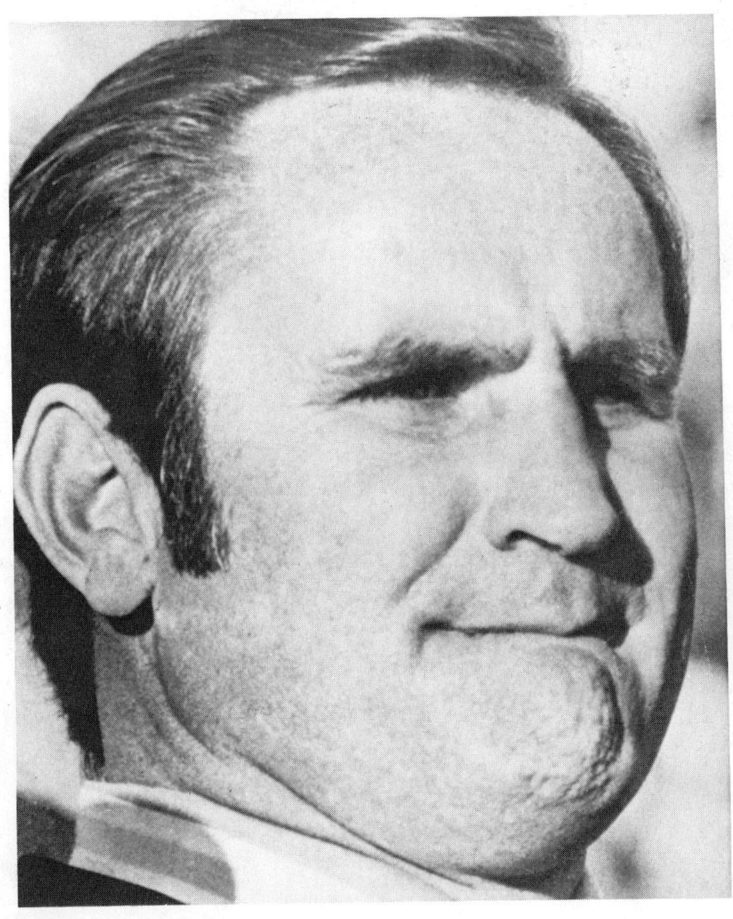

Watching his team go down to defeat, Don Shula bites his lip.

ONE FOR THE FLIPPER

Miami fans loyally defended Shula and the Dolphins. The coach had turned the team from cellar-dwellers into AFC champions in just two seasons. Wasn't that miracle enough?

Everyone but Don Shula agreed that it was.

The Miami Dolphins played their first game in 1966. They were an expansion team of the old American Football League, which later merged with the NFL.

Their first coach was George Wilson, former skipper of the Detroit Lions.

Their first mascot was a live Dolphin named Flipper, who dwelt in a pool at one end of their home stadium, the Orange Bowl.

Their first play in their first regular-season game was a 95-yard kickoff return resulting in a touchdown.

Joe Auer (left, center) became an instant hero by returning the kickoff 95 yards for a TD in the Dolphins' first home game, against Oakland.

George Wilson, first coach of the Dolphins, learns that one of his promising rookies, split end John Roderick, has suffered an injury that may put him out for the season. Injuries and bad luck plagued Coach Wilson, who was nonetheless instrumental in putting together the Dolphin team that later became one of football's all-time bests.

If only it had been an omen of great things to come! But the Dolphins lost that first game, 23-14, and they lost the next four games as well. Their first victory came in an exciting game against the Denver Broncos. Joe Auer fumbled and was responsible for a Denver touchdown. But he pulled himself out of the doghouse by scoring twice himself, the last TD coming less than 2 minutes before the end of the game. Miami won, 24-7.

There were only two more Miami wins that first season. The team tied with Houston for last place.

Rookie quarterback Bob Griese (12) prepares to pass in a 1967 game against the San Diego Chargers. The Dolphins suffered their seventh straight loss, going down 24-0.

Three important things are needed to build a truly great football team from scratch. The first is time. The second is good new players, secured from the draft or from trades. The third is the right kind of coaching to bring out the best in the team.

For the next three years, George Wilson coached the infant Dolphins, trying to make them winners. The team drafted Bob Griese, Larry Csonka, Jim Kiick, Dick Anderson, and other talented players. They traded for Nick Buoniconti, Larry Little, and Mercury Morris. Manny Fernandez, unwanted by other teams, signed as a free agent.

Larry Little,
All-Pro guard

Eugene "Mercury" Morris,
star rusher

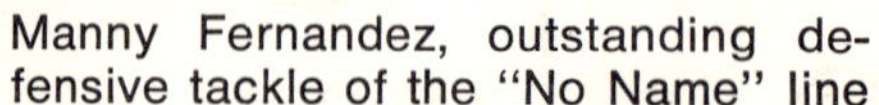

Manny Fernandez, outstanding defensive tackle of the "No Name" line

Nick Buoniconti, veteran linebacker and a leader of the Dolphin defense

They had talent and they had time. But the progress of the team seemed very slow. In 1967 they were 4-10-0. In 1968 they were 5-8-1. The team had yet to have a money-making season and the owners were very worried. The head of the Dolphin organization, Joe Robbie, told Coach Wilson that he would have to make the team a winner in 1969—or else.

But Wilson was unlucky. Many of his players suffered injuries and the rest hardly ever seemed to get it all together. The team finished with a terrible 3-10-1 record.

George Wilson was fired and Joe Robbie went looking for a miracle-worker who would be able to save the Miami Dolphins from ruin.

Joe Robbie (in glasses), managing general partner of the Dolphins, introduces his new coach, Don Shula.

Some jokers said that the team needed to bring back Flipper, the mascot who had retired in 1968.

But Joe Robbie knew the team needed more than a mascot. He hired Don Shula of the Baltimore Colts to be the new head coach at Miami.

Shula's Colts had lost Super Bowl III to the New York Jets after a 13-1-0 season in 1968. In 1969 the team slumped to 8-5-1, and the Colts' owner was very angry with Shula. The coach, in turn, was unhappy with the way the front office treated him. He was glad to go to Miami and make a fresh start.

THE FIRST SHULA YEAR

When Don Shula became the Dolphins' coach, he said:

"I am not a miracle-worker. I have no magic formulas. The only way I know is hard work."

Coach Shula was right about the hard work. But he was wrong about all the rest. There was a player's strike that year which cut short the training time before the exhibition games. With only six days to whip his men into shape, Shula came up with a miracle.

He made them practice four times a day in the hot Florida sun. He introduced a whole new system of plays designed to make the best use of quarterback Bob Griese. Several bright rookies won starting slots and the veterans shaped up under punishing training.

And the Dolphins, who had never won more than two games in a row, had four straight victories in the pre-season. The last was a 20-13 win over the division-champion New York Jets.

If it wasn't a miracle, it was close enough.

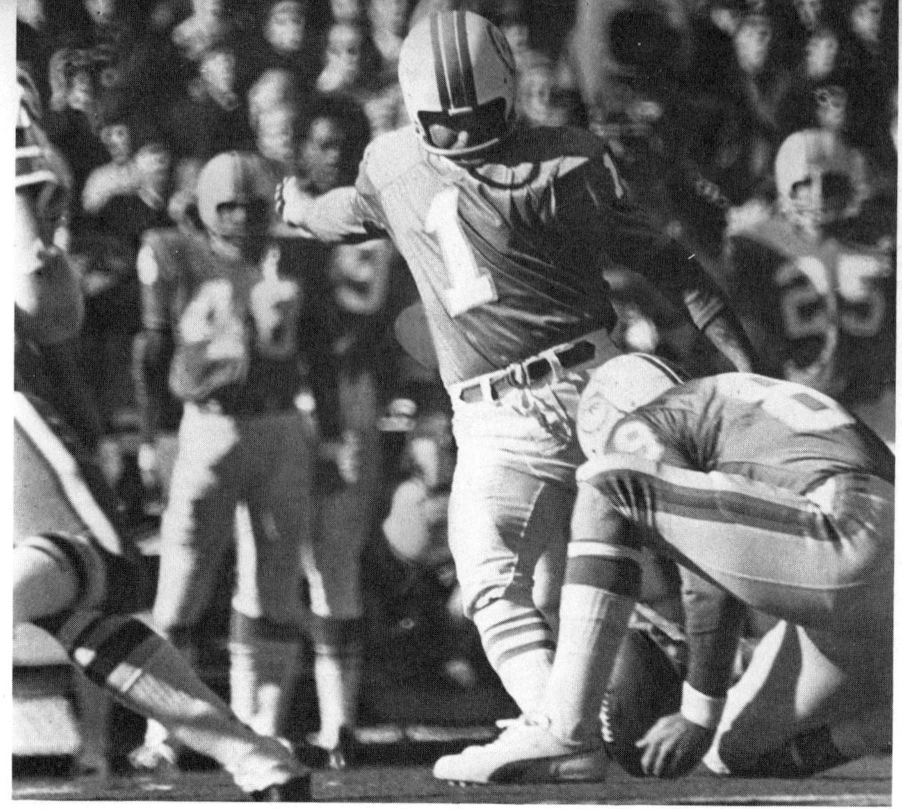

Garo Yepremian (1) was a European soccer player before becoming a top kicker. Karl Noonan holds.

They lost the next two exhibitions, as well as the season opener at Boston. Shula showed the team the fiery temper he was well-known for. Bob Griese had played especially badly, but Shula refused to bench him. He wanted to build up the young man's confidence.

Before the next game, against Houston, Shula added a new player to the Miami roster. He was Garo Yepremian, a short, balding native of Cyprus who had been a soccer player in Europe and later a field-goal kicker for the Detroit Lions.

Yepremian kicked two field goals in the Houston game. Griese connected for two touchdowns. The Dolphins won, 20-10.

Wide receiver Paul Warfield makes a successful grab.

Now Miami began to shine. A new receiver, Paul Warfield, made two touchdowns in the next game, against Oakland. Yepremian booted two more field goals and once again, Miami won.

The fourth game, against the Jets, was a hard-fought contest that challenged the Miami defense to hold back one of their toughest rivals. Joe Namath and the Jets were humiliated, 20-6, and the Dolphins felt like they were going into orbit. They were finally learning to win.

The Miami defense crushes Wayne Patrick of the Buffalo Bills. The Dolphins include John Richardson (74), Manny Fernandez (75), Jim Riley (70) and Ted Davis (54).

They played Buffalo, a very weak team, and racked up another victory, 33-14. Yepremian got four field goals this time.

A huge hometown crowd came out to see the next game, against Cleveland. And the Dolphins blew it, 28-0. The next game, against Shula's old team, the Colts, was even worse. The Dolphins sank without a trace, 35-0.

Shula felt like a man in a nightmare. The next week, Miami lost to Philadelphia, 24-17. Bob Griese had been taken out of the game in the last period. Sub quarterback John Stofa earned the 17 points. Fans began to urge Shula to bench Griese.

Bob Griese makes a call.

But the coach refused. He knew Griese had great ability and gambled that a display of confidence would lift the quarterback up.

Miami played New Orleans, and won. Griese played a game that the coach pronounced to be "practically perfect."

But the biggest challenge, the real prover, came the following week. Miami had a rematch with the Baltimore Colts, who were leading the Eastern Division.

It was a wild game. Baltimore got on the board first with a field goal. Then rookie defensive back Jake Scott of the Dolphins took a punt 77 yards for a touchdown. Miami led, 7-3. Bob Griese showed what he was made of by marshaling an 80-yard drive. On third and 14, he ran for a score himself on a quarterback draw play.

The Colts fought back but the momentum belonged to Miami. They won, 34-17. Later, Shula said: "I knew that we had begun to turn things around."

And it was true. They won the remaining four games of the season for a remarkable 10-4-0 record. More than 70,000 happy fans saw the last regular game against the Buffalo Bills. It turned out to be the biggest win ever for the Dolphins—45-7.

The playoff was against the tough Oakland Raiders on California turf. Shula knew that the odds were against his young team playing these hard-bitten veterans. And he was right. The Dolphins bowed, 21-14, but they played a good game.

When it was over, Coach Shula said: "Gentlemen, I appreciate your effort."

In a rugged playoff game, Bob Griese is mauled by Oakland Raider defensive end Ben Davidson.

FOOTBALL'S LONGEST GAME

The 1971 season was to be one of great highs and deep lows. It saw Bob Griese and Paul Warfield become football's hottest passing combo, while Garo Yepremian was king of the field goals.

It saw Jim Kiick and Larry Csonka labeled "Butch Cassidy and the Sundance Kid" after holding out for higher salaries. Later, the pair trampled their way to backfield stardom.

The season had a slow start and a fast finish. After dropping some early contests, Miami came on strong. They trailed Baltimore by half a game in the 13th week, then unexpectedly became Eastern Division champs when the Colts were upset by the lowly New England Patriots.

The Dolphins won their last game, against Green Bay, and finished 10-3-1.

Larry Csonka leads interference for Jim Kiick.

The highest point of the season came during the AFC championship game against the Kansas City Chiefs. The game has gone down in history as "football's longest day."

Kansas City scored twice in the first period with a field goal and a touchdown. In the second quarter, Miami bounced back. Griese engineered a touchdown drive with Csonka making the score. Then, in the last minute of the half, Yepremian evened the score with a field goal.

In the second half, Kansas City controlled the ball for over 9 minutes, coming up with another touchdown. The Chiefs led, 17-10.

Griese took over and hit on four passes out of four. On the last, Jim Kiick went over the goal-line. Little Yepremian booted the extra point and it was 17-17.

In the fourth period, a big play by Kansas City's Elmo Wright took the ball 63 yards to the Miami 3. The Chiefs went over on the next play. With a good kick, the Chiefs went ahead, 24-17.

Following the block of guard Bob Kuechenberg (67), Csonka goes for a 2-yard touchdown in football's "longest game."

Six and a half minutes remained in the period. Refusing to panic, the Dolphins moved coolly down the field. Griese connected twice in critical third-down plays, bringing them to the Kansas City 12. Two minutes were left and a field goal wouldn't help them.

Griese passed to Twilley on the 5. Now the Dolphin line strained to hold back the Chiefs from the quarterback as he let fly the ball.

Marv Fleming scooped it in. Touchdown! And the kick was good. The score stood at 24-24.

Yepremian kicked off in the last minute. And Kansas City almost got the biggest play of the game. Ed Podolak of the Chiefs took the ball and ran unhindered toward the Miami end zone. All that stood between him and a score were Garo Yepremian and Curtis Johnson.

Kickers are not supposed to attack. But Garo went after Podolak and forced him to change his direction. As the crowd screamed, Johnson brought Podolak down and saved the game.

The ball was on Miami's 22. Miraculously, the Chiefs' great kicker, Jan Stenerud, missed a field-goal attempt by inches.

The game went into sudden-death overtime.

In the fifth period, the Chiefs got to within field-goal range again. Fans held their breath as Stenerud kicked—but Miami's Nick Buoniconti gave a mighty leap and blocked it.

Then it was the Dolphins' turn. Yepremian tried for a heroic 52-yard boot and failed. The fifth period ended and the sixth began.

The Chiefs expected Griese to hand off to Kiick. Instead, he called a "roll right, trap left" to Csonka, who ran for 29 yards to the KC 36. They bought a few more yards, then called on Yepremian.

Bob DeMarco made a perfect snap. Karl Noonan held it and Garo kicked right down the middle. The ball soared into the night sky. Football's longest game, 82 minutes and 40 seconds, was over.

Miami had won, 27-24. They were AFC champs, on their way to Super Bowl VI.

THE PERFECT SEASON

Don Shula was bitterly disappointed when his Dolphins lost Super Bowl VI to the Baltimore Colts. He was being called a miracle man, but he would never be satisfied until his team was the world champion.

Before the 1972 season opened, Shula took out some "quarterback insurance." He hired veteran QB Earl Morrall from the Colts as a backup for Griese. Young Colt players teased Morrall, who at 38 was an "old man" by pro football standards. They even put a rocker by his locker!

Morrall had the last laugh. The Dolphins won the first four games with Griese as starter. But in the fifth game, against the San Diego Chargers, the talented young quarterback broke his ankle. Earl Morrall came in and turned the scoreless contest into a 24-10 victory for Miami.

Griese would be out for the rest of the regular season. During that time, Morrall quarterbacked nine more winning games for Miami. They finished 14-0-0, the first team ever to do so. It was the first perfect season since the Chicago Bears had won all eleven regular games in 1942.

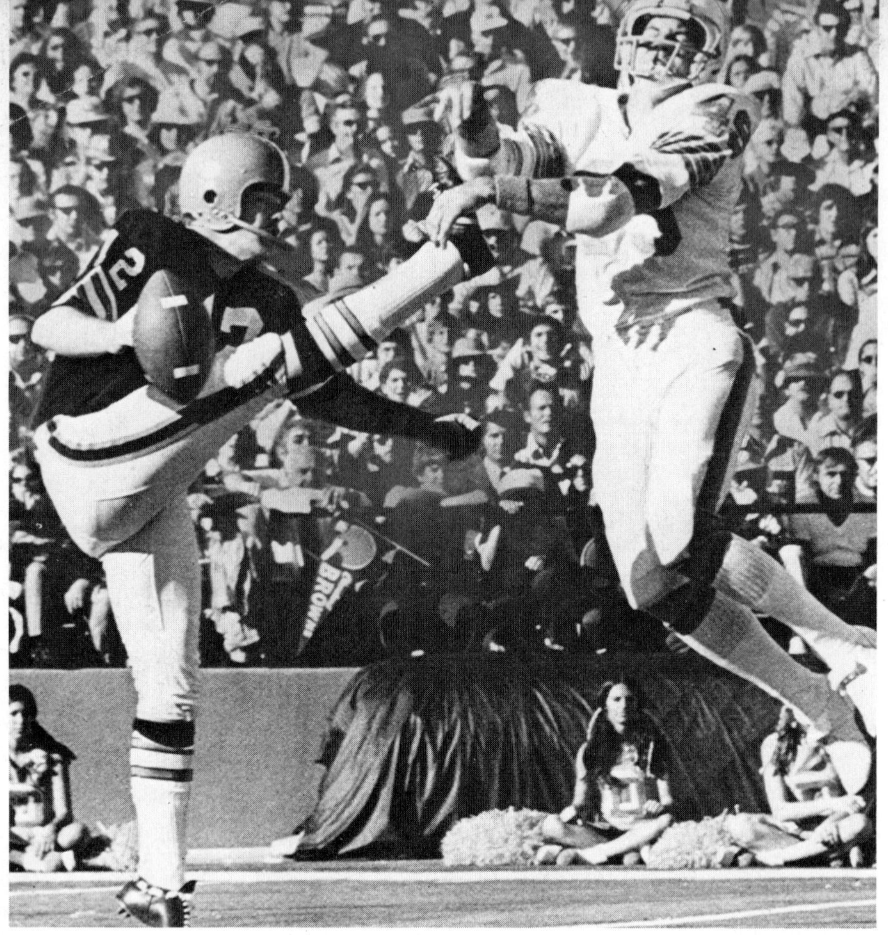

Miami Safety Charles Babb (49) blocks a punt attempt by Cleveland's Don Cockcroft during the 1972 playoff. Babb ran the ball for a touchdown.

The first playoff put the Dolphins up against the "wild card" Cleveland Browns. With only eight minutes left, Cleveland led by 14-13. It had been the Dolphin's toughest game of the year. The offense was feeling the strain and most of the credit for keeping Miami alive belonged to its valiant "No-Name" defense.

But Earl Morrall reached into his bag of tricks and came up with one more. In just seven plays he marched his tired troops 80 yards for the winning touchdown. The final score was 20-14.

Facing the Steelers for the 1972 AFC title, the Dolphins experienced trouble in the first half. Coach Shula sent in Bob Griese (12) in the second half. Other players are Jim Kiick (21), Garo Yepremian (1) and Al Jenkins (60).

Now they played the AFC title game, against the Pittsburgh Steelers. Bob Griese was now fully recovered. When Morrall had trouble moving the offense, Don Shula sent Griese in for the second half. The score was tied, 7-7.

The Steelers got a field goal. It was 10-7. Then Griese took over. He drove the Dolphins 80 yards for a TD. In the fourth quarter, ten running plays culminated in another touchdown by Jim Kiick. Then Pittsburgh scored again—but the Steelers could do no more. The "No-Name" defense intercepted two of their passes, wrapping up a 21-17 victory for the Dolphins.

Sixteen wins in a row! And the seventeenth Sunday was Super Bowl VII, to be played against the Washington Redskins.

Shula had planned the game carefully, starting Griese and coaching his defense on the way to contain Redskin star running back Larry Brown.

And the Dolphins did things right. The No-Names bottled up Brown. In the last part of the first period, Griese got a successful drive going. He hit paydirt in the last minute on a 28-yard pass to Howard Twilley for a touchdown. With the point, Miami led, 7-0.

In Washington's next series, Dolphin Jake Scott intercepted. The two teams battled back and forth, well matched, until the last two minutes of the half. Then Miami's brilliant Nick Buoniconti intercepted and ran the ball to the Redskin 27.

Jim Kiick went up the middle for 3 yards. Larry Csonka bought a few more. Then Griese passed to Jim Mandich, who was downed on the Washington 2.

With only seconds remaining, Kiick tried to get through. Failure. On the next attempt, All-Pro guard Larry Little scattered the Redskin defense and Kiick scored a touchdown. With the point, Miami led, 14-0 at the half.

The third quarter was scoreless. Miami star tackle Manny Fernandez had a big play when he dumped Redskin QB Billy Kilmer, spoiling a TD drive. Washington tried for a field goal and missed. Griese wound up the Miami offense, only to see it all amount to nothing when a touchdown pass was intercepted in the end zone.

In the last quarter, one of the strangest and funniest of all Super Bowl plays occurred. Garo Yepremian tried for a 42-yard field goal and Washington blocked the kick. The ball bounced back toward the little kicker. But instead of falling on it, Yepremian picked it up and tried to pass!

On the sidelines, Don Shula howled in dismay. Mike Bass of the Redskins intercepted the puny toss and ran it all the way for a touchdown. Poor Yepremian, who had pulled so many Miami games out of the fire in the past, had to slink off the field in disgrace as Washington kicked the extra point.

Two minutes were left. The Redskins tried hard, but the stars smiled on the Miami Dolphins that day. They rushed the Redskin quarterback, then rode out the clock.

At ease for a moment during Super Bowl VII are Miami defenders Bob Matheson, Manny Fernandez, and Doug Swift.

Earl Morrall stares horror-stricken at Garo Yepremian as the kicker tries to turn quarterback and passes weakly. Redskin cornerback Mike Bass (41) leaps for the interception, which he ran all the way for a touchdown.

And the Miami Dolphins were Super Bowl winners by a score of 14-7. The perfect season had a perfect ending, with Don Shula carried off the field by his jubilant players.

"Nobody," he said, "has done what my team has done. As far as I'm concerned, this is the finest team I've ever seen, either as a coach or a player."

Millions of football fans all over the nation had to agree.

Don Shula and Vince Lombardi separate after the traditional game-ending handshake in 1965, when Shula was coach of the Colts. The expressions on the faces of the coaches reveal which team won.

SUPER BOWL VIII

More than any other man, Don Shula had admired the late coach of the Green Bay Packers, Vince Lombardi. Both men drove their teams hard, believing that hard work produced championships. Both took losing football clubs and turned them into winners.

After Super Bowl VII, many people began comparing Shula to Lombardi, and the Dolphins to the great Green Bay team of the middle '60's that had won Super Bowls I and II.

Just before the 1973 season, Don Shula said: "We'd like to win back-to-back Super Bowls, which no team has done since Green Bay. And we'd like to write some new history as far as winning is concerned."

The last part of his hope was not to be. Miami could not quite manage a second perfect season. They had to settle for 12-2-0.

The AFC championship game was played against the Oakland Raiders, an ancient foe of the Dolphins which had been responsible for one of Miami's 1973 losses. Could Oakland do it again?

The Dolphins won the toss and elected to receive. Eight plays brought Miami to the Oakland 11. From there Csonka rumbled over for the first touchdown.

It was an omen of things to come. Csonka scored two more TD's in that game. Nothing Oakland tried was able to stop him. Chugging along behind Larry Little, he seemed to shed tacklers like a human tank.

Miami won, 27-10, and went to the Super Bowl for the third time.

Larry Csonka, the human battering ram, flies close to the ground during the 1973 AFC title game against Oakland. Looming above Csonka is the Raiders' Otis Sistrunk (60).

Super Bowl VIII matched the Miami Dolphins against the Minnesota Vikings. It was a tough game to predict. Minnesota had one of football's best quarterbacks, Fran Tarkenton, and a splendid set of defenders nicknamed the Purple People Eaters.

Miami had the ball first. Griese stayed mostly on the ground as he took the offense downfield. Both Csonka and Mercury Morris shared the rushing chores.

Nine quick plays took Miami to the Minnesota 8. There Griese sent Larry Little and Bob Kuechenberg off to the right, decoying the Viking defense and creating a hole for Csonka. He went through for a touchdown.

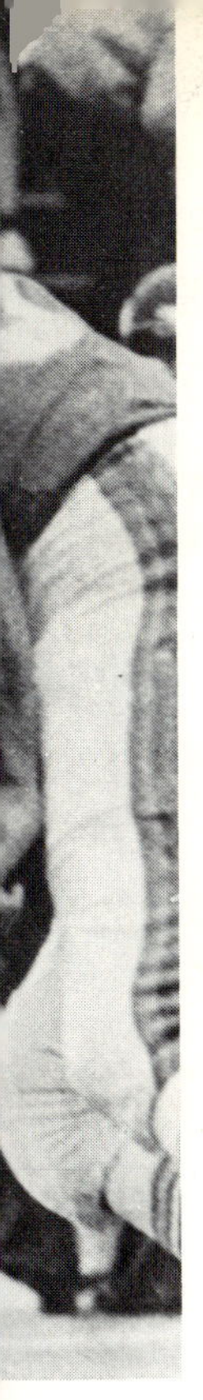

Super Bowl VIII starts out with a Miami touchdown drive as Griese pulls away from center and prepares to hand off to Csonka.

Minnesota gained only 9 yards on its next series and had to punt. Miami took over and once again proved superior to the hapless Purple defense. It took seven plays for them to reach the Viking 14. There Griese passed to wide receiver Marlin Briscoe for 13 yards. And Jim Kiick bulled over from the 1.

Miami led, 14-0, at the end of the first quarter.

Minnesota stiffened somewhat in the next period, but the Dolphins still managed a field goal. Then Tarkenton finally got a good drive going. The Vikings went all the way to the Miami 6—but there Oscar Reed fumbled and Dolphin Nick Buoniconti recovered.

When the half ended, Miami led, 17-0.

The third period brought new disaster to Minnesota. After only four plays they had to punt. Griese went to Morris and Csonka for short gains, then hit Warfield for 27 yards.

A defensive holding penalty against the Vikings brought the Dolphins to the Minnesota 8. The mighty Csonka trucked into the end zone two plays later. Yepremian's kick was good and it was 24-0.

Fran Tarkenton tried hard. He got a good drive going and finally took the ball over the goal-line himself for Minnesota's one lone touchdown, in the fourth quarter. But the Dolphin magic was not to be denied.

At the end, the score was 24-7. And the Dolphins had won their second Super Bowl in a row.

The outstanding player of Super Bowl VIII was Larry Csonka, who seems unstoppable as he crashes through a mass of frustrated Vikings.

NFL Commissioner Pete Rozelle and owner Joe Robbie congratulate Don Shula, who holds the Vince Lombardi Trophy after leading his players to their second Super Bowl victory in 1974.

Larry Csonka had had an incredible day, rushing 145 yards in 33 carries. People began comparing him to the immortal Jim Brown. As for the rest of the Dolphins. . .

Coach Don Shula, the two-time Super Winner, summed it up. He said: "It's not for me to say our team is the best of all time. But I'd like to say this about my football team. In the four years I've been coach, we've gotten better every year. And winning the Super Bowl back-to-back is something only the Packers ever did before. I just couldn't be prouder of this team."

MIAMI DOLPHINS

The first pro football team in Miami was the Seahawks of the old AAFC, which played only a single season, in 1946, before the franchise was transferred to Baltimore. The Dolphins were born in 1966 in an expansion of the American Football League. In 1970 they became part of the Eastern Division of the American Conference of the reorganized NFL.

RECORD

Year	Won	Lost	Tied	Pct.
1966	3	11	0	.214
1967	4	10	0	.286
1968	5	8	1	.385
1969	3	10	1	.231
1970	10	4	0	.714
1971	10	3	1	.769
1972	14	0	0	1.000
1973	12	2	0	.857